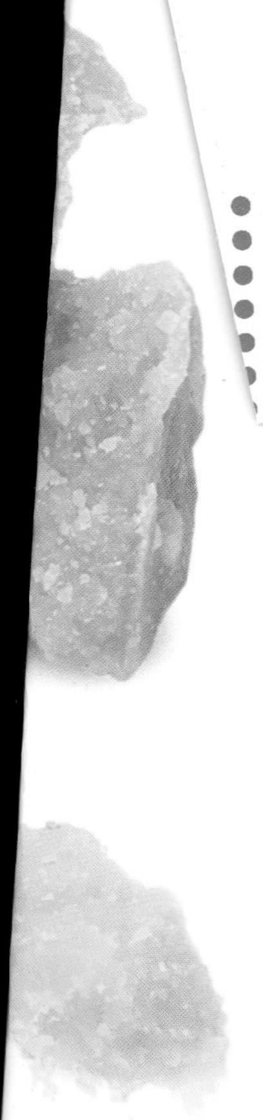

CREATED BY
ACADEMIA BARILLA

PHOTOGRAPHY BY
**ALBERTO ROSSI
CHEF MARIO STROLLO**

RECIPES BY
CHEF MARIO GRAZIA

TEXT BY
MARIAGRAZIA VILLA

GRAPHIC DESIGN
MARINELLA DEBERNARDI

EDITORIAL COORDINATION ACADEMIA BARILLA
**CHATO MORANDI
ILARIA ROSSI
BECKY PICKRELL**

CONTENTS

4

5

THE BIG CHEESE (FOR AT LEAST NINE CENTURIES!)

There was a mountain there, of pure grated Parmigiano cheese, on which stood men who did nothing else but make macaroni and ravioli and cook them in capon broth, and then throw them down; and the more one grabbed, the more one got.

Giovanni Boccaccio, *The Decameron*, VIII 3, 1351

Parmigiano Reggiano, is the pride and joy of Italian cuisine. Known, appreciated, and imitated throughout the world. The complete cheese. The one that satisfies both the delicate and the strong palate, that is relished alone or in dishes, that is adapted, on both a daily basis and creatively, to either the prose or poetry of the table. A masterpiece of the art of dairy farming for at least nine centuries, created without any preservatives. A treasure chest of fragrance and aroma with a glorious gastronomic history. An important ally in a healthy diet with nutrients of supreme value.

The Identity of the King of Cheese

Real Parmigiano Reggiano bears its identity card on its body: the classic dotted script with its name and the stamps with its date of production, the alpha-numeric identification code of the individual object, and the number of the relevant dairy factory. Made with cow's milk and the sole addition of rennet, fire, and the wisdom of the dairyman, it is placed in a cylindrical cheese-mold, in which it assumes a form, immersed in a salt-water bath, and is then aged for a minimum of 12 to as many as 36 or more months. During the 12th month, inspectors from the Consortium check each cheese to make sure that it meets the standards required to be branded and become the prized cheese with its typical pale straw-colored granular structure that flakes when broken and can be used either at the table or grated after a second phase of ripening.

Opening and Preserving

Parmigiano Reggiano should not be cut. In order to retains its granularity, it should be opened with the traditional knife, one with a short, pointy, almond-shaped blade. Prepackaged and vacuum-packed, it can be stored in a refrigerator (but not frozen) for several months. Once unpackaged or cut directly from the whole cheese, its quality will keep for approximately 15 days to a month, depending on its age. It is important to keep the cheese at a temperature between 39 and 40°F, in the optimal humidity level of a vegetable bin, apart from other foods so that it does not absorb odors, and stored inside a plastic or glass container or covered in food wrap.

Natural Nutrition

A veritable concentrate of nutrients: 17 quarts (16 liters) of high-grade milk are needed to produce 2 pounds (1 kilo) of Parmigiano Reggiano. Thanks to the skimming of the evening milk, this cheese is packed with protein and minerals, particularly calcium, but also phosphorus, potassium, magnesium, and zinc, as well as vitamins, such as A, B6, and B2. The additional benefit of easy digestibility makes it particularly suitable for children, athletes, and the elderly.

Irreplaceable in the Kitchen

Many people—particularly the French, have a weakness for Parmigiano Reggiano. It is said that the playwright Molière asked for a little piece of the delicious cheese at the moment of his death, perhaps in order to close his successful career in a beautiful manner. The writer Alexandre Dumas père, was crazy about macaroni with meat sauce and so much Parmigiano Reggiano that according to his guests, he served cheese with macaroni and meat sauce. Even Emperor Napoleon Bonaparte would pass up any delicacy for a simple plate of green beans with macaroni and meat sauce. Even Emperor Napoleon Reggiano flakes. The versatility of this cheese in the kitchen is supreme. Academia Barilla, the international center devoted to the diffusion of Italian cuisine across the world, has selected 50 extravagant manners in which to savor it. From light and aromatic appetizers, grated over a first course or soup, in egg dishes, carpaccio, meat and fish entrées, and vegetable sides, to breads, crackers, breadsticks, and unusual snacks.

PARMIGIANO REGGIANO: THE "KING" OF CHEESE

Before Parmigiano Reggiano

The history of the cheese from Parma is long and complex. It began in what is now Bologna, with the Etruscans who, in the area around Parma, certainly bred sheep and goats, from whose milk they made a hard cheese meant to be grated. In the Roman era, cheeses produced in the region of Parma were known and prized in the Imperial capital, where they arrived via the port of Luni. It was there, before being loaded aboard, that they were branded with the sign of the moon. This is the earliest clear record of a cheese being marked according to its origin and appreciated as such by the Romans.

The "technology" of Parmigiano Reggiano

After the fall of the Roman empire, the agricultural revolution led by monks in the territory of Parma at the turn of the 11th century, which resulted in the reclamation of vast areas of swampy land and the expansion of stable pastures, led to the spread of cattle-breeding and the use of cow's milk. Thus the cheese formerly made of sheep's or goat's milk came first to be mixed with cow's milk but later exclusively made from it. In step with this development, the size of the molds and the length of the aging process increased. Since the earliest known secure documents referring to Parmigiano Reggiano date to 1254, we may reasonably assume that the technology used to produce it was already clearly defined in the previous century. Through careful observation and experimentation, the monks succeeded in systematizing the milk drawn in the evening, which they skimmed, with morning milk, which they left whole. The reduced fat content granted them better control over bacterial activity, reduced the risk of fermentation, and endowed this cheese—a veritable "preserver of milk"—a longevity that lasted years. The same exact technology that has remained basically untouched for centuries.

The Land of Cockaigne

In the mid-14th century, the Florentine writer Giovanni Boccaccio (1313-1375) notes in *The Decameron* the use of

Parmigiano for seasoning macaroni and ravioli, which he describes in the "Land of Cockaigne" and grants a character and fame that has remained unchanged to this day. One must not overlook the "Boccaccian" reference to Parmigiano in a novel written in 1399 by Giovanni Sercambi (1348-1424) of Lucca, set in the countryside of Parma itself. Besides being the principal manufacturer, Parma was also the marketing center of the molded cheeses that soon began to be exported to other Italian states as well as throughout Europe. In the 15th century, the largest dairy entrepreneur was the convent of San Giovanni, with its four active cheese factories: two near Parma, in Gainago and Beneceto, and two in Reggiano, in Cadè and in Cadelbosco di Sopra.

Even the most important noble families began to invest in the production of cheese. Generally the cheese factory was annexed to a dairy farm, but not all owners had the means to maintain a large herd; they often had to limit themselves to a stable with 10-20 heads of cattle, whose milk was added to that produced in the stalls of tenant farmers. These, in turn, usually owned one to three cows per household and assisted the cheese-maker, later receiving cheese after handing over enough milk to manufacture one or more molds. The cheese maker was called the "turnario" and in subsequent centuries came to work even without a dairy farm.

The First Designation of Origin: 1612

It is to the lucky intuition of the Duke of Parma, Ranuccio I Farnese (1569-1622), that we owe the first document that officially designates the cheese as "Parmigiano" and which was signed by the notary of the Ducal Chamber on August 7, 1612. Parmigiano cheese is also mentioned by Vicenzo Tanara (16th century – 1669) in his treatise on the economic management of the private villa, first published in Bologna in 1644 and destined to become a great publishing success.

After a century of slow but progressive economic decline, the quantity and quality of the cheese produced in Parma declined. On the other hand, the cheese produced in Reggiano "held up" remarkably well. With the rise of

9

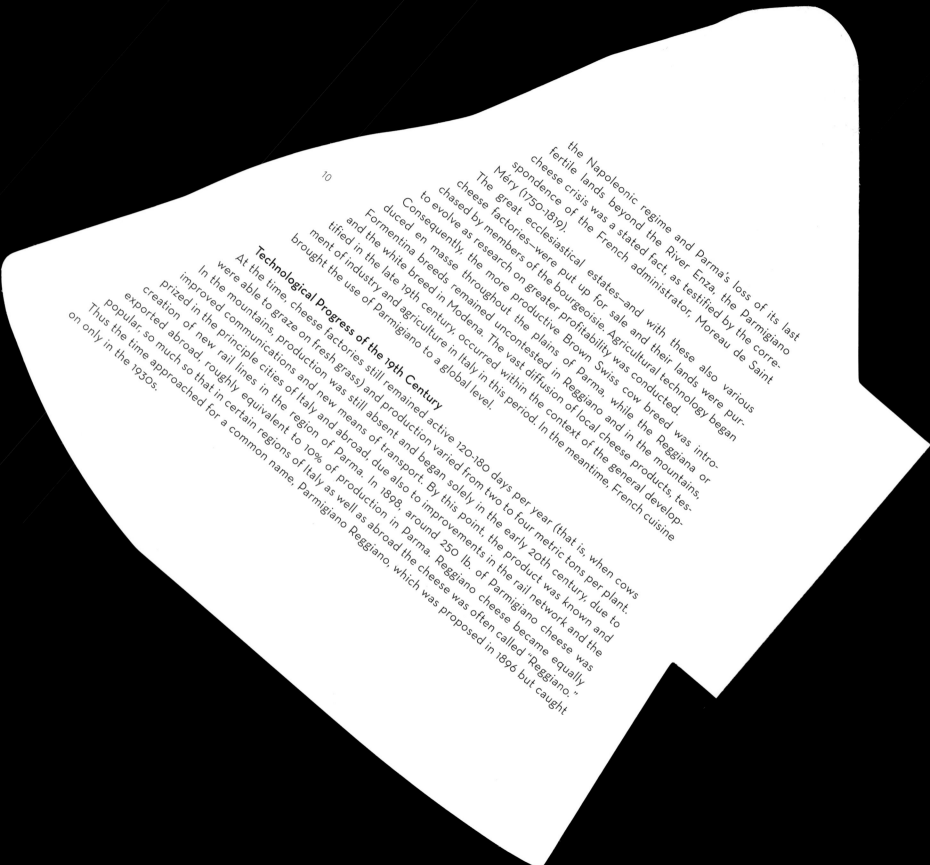

the Napoleonic regime and Parma's loss of its last fertile lands beyond the River Enza, the Parmigiano cheese crisis was a stated fact, as testified by the correspondence of the French administrator, Moreau de Saint Méry (1750-1819).

The great ecclesiastical estates—and with these also various cheese factories—were put up for sale and their lands were purchased by members of the bourgeoisie. Agricultural technology began to evolve as research on greater profitability was conducted.

Consequently, the more productive Brown Swiss cow breed was introduced en masse throughout the plains of Parma, while the Reggiana or Formentina breed in Modena. The vast diffusion of local cheese products, testified in the late 19th century, occurred within the context of the general development of industry and agriculture in Italy in this period. In the meantime, French cuisine brought the use of Parmigiano to a global level.

Technological Progress of the 19th Century

At the time, cheese factories still remained active 120-180 days per year (that is, when cows were able to graze on fresh grass) and production varied from two to four metric tons per plant.

In the mountains, production was still absent and began solely in the early 20th century, due to improved communications and new means of transport. By this point, the product was known and prized in the principle cities of Italy and abroad, due also to improvements in the rail network and the creation of new rail lines in the region of Parma. In 1898, around 250 lb. of Parmigiano cheese was exported abroad, roughly equivalent to 10% of production in Parma. Reggiano cheese became equally popular, so much so that in certain regions of Italy as well as abroad the cheese was often called "Reggiano." Thus the time approached for a common name, Parmigiano Reggiano, which was proposed in 1896 but caught on only in the 1930s.

The transformation of the cheese had reached a fairly high technological level by the 19th century, but the ratio of waste was still great enough to render production economically insecure; a technological shift thus became necessary but was achieved only in the early twentieth century with the spread of steam heat, whey-starter culture, and curd-breaking, thanks to the fundamental contribution of the experimentation and development carried out by the Zenelli Institute in Reggio Emilia.

A Consortium to Supervise Quality

In 1934, the Consorzio del Formaggio Parmigiano Reggiano was founded in Reggio Emilia in order to brand and distinguish the production of authentic Parmigiano Reggiano. In 1937, the district of production was defined according to borders still intact today, and in 1938 the term "Parmigiano Reggiano" became official for the first time.

After the reconstruction, starting in the 1950s, the production of Parmigiano Reggiano underwent a further robust development.

Today the Consorzio del Formaggio Parmigiano Reggiano, founded in 1954 and born of the old Consorzio Volontario Interprovinciale, established in Reggio Emilia in 1934, integrates the cheese manufacturers of the same name in the provinces of Parma, Reggio Emilia, Modena, Mantua (on the right bank of the Po), and Bologna (on the left bank of the Reno), which constitute the typical area of production, guarantees the quality of the product, and ensures it is obtained with artisinal labor techniques that have not changed in nine centuries.

The name Parmigiano Reggiano was granted the European Union's official seal of protection DOP in 1996, and today the cheese is considered the "king" of cheese due to its organoleptic qualities and method of production.

Giancarlo Gonizzi
Curator of the Biblioteca Gastronomica di Academia Barilla

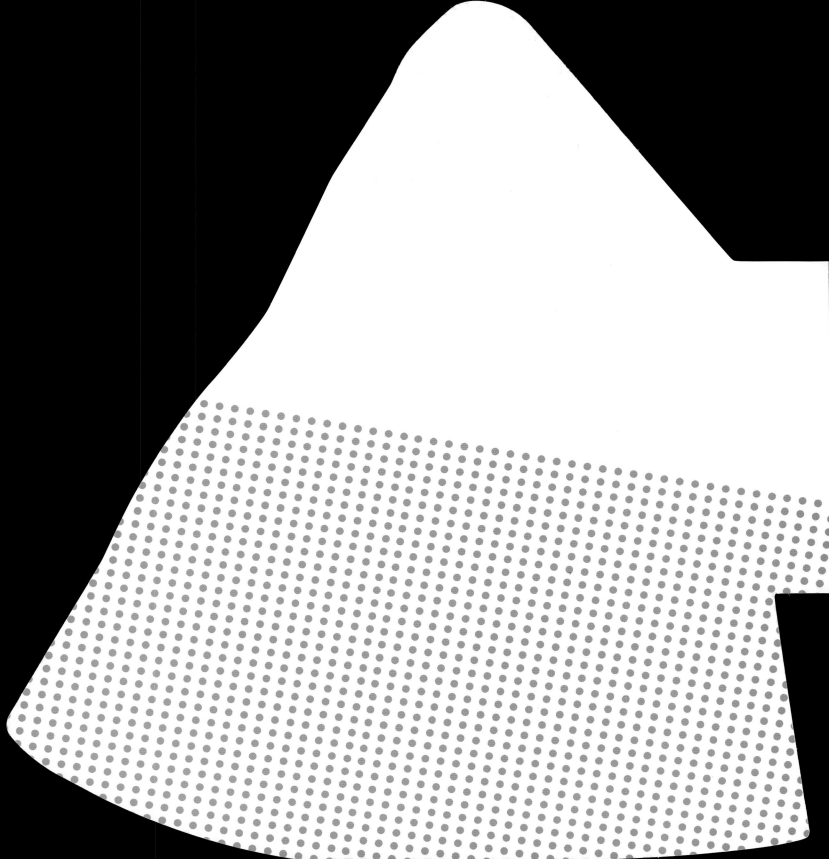

APPETIZERS

NUT ENCRUSTED ARANCINI

INGREDIENTS FOR 4 PEOPLE

For the arancini
9 oz. (250 g) rice
4 1/4 cups (1 L) beef broth
1 egg
2 tbsp. (30 g) butter
3 1/2 oz. (100 g)
Parmigiano Reggiano
cheese, grated
Salt

For the breading
1/4 cup (50 g) flour
3 eggs, beaten
3/4 cup (150 g) breadcrumbs
3 1/2 oz. (100 g) hazelnuts, ground

Oil, for frying
Traditional balsamic vinegar
from Modena (optional)

METHOD

Cook the rice *al dente* in the beef broth. Drain it, and add in the egg, butter, and grated Parmigiano Reggiano, mixing to a creamy consistency. Adjust the flavor with salt, and let cool.
Shape the rice into little balls. Roll them first in the flour, then the beaten eggs, and finally in the breadcrumb and ground hazelnut mixture. Deep fry the arancini in oil.
Serve as desired with a drizzle of traditional balsamic vinegar from Modena.

DID YOU KNOW...

Arancini are one of the great classics of Sicilian cuisine. They come in many versions in the island's many fried-food shops: with meat sauce, with prosciutto and peas, with mozzarella, ricotta, spinach... They can also assume different shapes, but most of the time they look like little oval or elongated pears. They are enjoyed, hot and fragrant, as little timbales on the go, just right for sating the appetite in a pleasant and light manner, but also as an antipasto, a first or main course. Similar to Sicilian arancini, are the rice *supplì* of the Roman tradition, also known as the "*supplì al telefono*" because they are stuffed with mozzarella, and when broken in half, the melted cheese stretches into a cord between the two pieces. In order to produce this amusing effect, they need to be enjoyed while very hot.

Preparation time: 30' - Cooking time: 20'
Difficulty: medium

PASTRY-PUFFS WITH PARMIGIANO REGGIANO CREAM

INGREDIENTS FOR 4 PEOPLE

For the puffs
1/2 cup (100 ml) water
3 1/2 tbsp. (50 g) butter
2 oz. (60 g) flour
2 eggs
Salt

For the Parmigiano Reggiano cream
1 egg
3 egg yolks
2 tsp. (10 g) flour
1 cup (250 ml) milk, scalded
2 1/4 oz. (60 g) Parmigiano Reggiano cheese, grated
1 tbsp. (15 g) butter
Salt

METHOD

To prepare the puffs, boil the water in a saucepan with the butter and a pinch of salt. Add the flour and cook until the mixture pulls away from the sides of the pan. Remove from heat and add the eggs, little by little, mixing well. Using a pastry bag, shape the dough into puffs on a baking sheet lined with parchment paper. Bake at 375 oF (190 °C) for approximately 15 minutes.

To prepare the Parmigiano Reggiano cream, whisk the egg and the yolks with salt to taste in a saucepan. Add the flour and scalded milk. Bring to a boil and let boil for 2-3 minutes. Remove from heat and add the cheese and butter.

Use a pastry bag to fill the puffs with the Parmigiano Reggiano cream. Serve warm.

Preparation time: 40' - Cooking time: 15'
Difficulty: medium

CHEESE
TOAST

INGREDIENTS FOR 4 PEOPLE

3 1/2 oz. (100 g) Parmigiano Reggiano cheese, grated
4 tbsp. (60 ml) extra-virgin olive oil
1/2 tbsp. (7 ml) grappa
Pepper, freshly ground
8 slices of white bread

METHOD

Mix the grated Parmigiano Reggiano, olive oil, grappa, and pepper in a bowl, and refrigerate for at least an hour.
Toast the bread slices in the oven, using the broiler setting, until they are nicely browned.
Spread the toasted bread with the Parmigiano Reggiano mixture and serve immediately.

DID YOU KNOW...

The earliest cheese-makers, or rather people assigned to working, preparing, and storing dairy products, seem to go back to the civilization of Sumer, that is, to the third millennium BC. It was the ones who worked in ancient Rome, however, who introduced the use of cow's milk for the production of cheese and who perfected dairy techniques and related tools. Many of their procedures, such as the weighing of milk, addition of rennet, cream-skimming, and setting forms, have remained nearly unchanged. This is equally true of the instruments, such as the skimmer, the large wooden ladle used to skim the milk; the curd knife, given this name because it originally consisted of a bundle of hawthorn branches used to break up the curds in the cauldron; or the churn, a wooden container shaped either like a cylinder or a truncated cone and used to whip the cream and transform it into butter.

Preparation time: 10' - Cooking time: 10'
Resting time: 1 h - Difficulty: easy

REGGIO-STYLE COOKED GREENS

INGREDIENTS FOR 4 PEOPLE

For the pasta
1/3 lb. (150 g) flour
1 tbsp. (15 g) butter
Seltzer water
Salt

For the filling
18 oz. (500 g) Swiss chard
9 oz. (250 g) spinach

3 1/2 oz. (100 g) onion
1 clove garlic, finely minced
1 1/2 oz. (40 g) lard
Nutmeg to taste
Breadcrumbs, as needed
1 3/4 oz. (50 g) Parmigiano
Reggiano cheese, grated
Salt

METHOD

Knead the flour with the butter and seltzer water on a pastry board. Add the salt, and continue kneading until the dough is smooth and uniform.

Clean and rinse the greens and cook them with the onion and minced garlic, which have been fried in three-quarters of the lard. If necessary, drain the greens, then add a pinch of nutmeg, the bread crumbs, Parmigiano Reggiano, and salt until the filling is rather dense.

Divide the dough into two parts, one slightly larger than the other. Using a rolling pin, roll out the larger portion until it is fairly thin, and then lay it out on a greased baking sheet. Spread a layer of the filling (not too thick) over the dough and top everything with another layer of fairly thin, rolled-out dough. Dot the surface with bits of lard and pierce all over with a fork.

Bake at 390 ºF (200 ºC) for around 30 minutes.

Preparation time: 1 h - Cooking time: 30'
Difficulty: medium

PARMIGIANO REGGIANO FONDUE

INGREDIENTS FOR 4 PEOPLE

For the fondue
2 1/2 tbsp. (35 g) butter
2 1/2 tbsp. (35 g) flour
2/3 cup (150 ml) milk
7 oz. (200 g) Parmigiano Reggiano cheese, grated
Salt

For the breading
1/4 cup (50 g) flour
2 eggs, beaten
1/2 cup (100 g) breadcrumbs

Oil, for frying

METHOD

Melt the butter in a saucepan, and then stir in the flour. Cook for a few minutes without letting the mixture brown.

Add the milk, bring to a boil, and cook for a minute or two. Remove from heat and let cool. Add the grated Parmigiano Reggiano, and salt to taste, if necessary.

Spread the fondue over a greased plate and let chill. Cut up into regular pieces (circles, squares, or diamonds). Dip the pieces in the flour, then in the beaten eggs, and finally in the breadcrumbs.

Deep fry in very hot oil, drain on paper towels, and serve immediately.

Preparation time: 1 h - Cooking time: 2-4'
Difficulty: medium

ARTICHOKE SALAD WITH PARMIGIANO REGGIANO

INGREDIENTS FOR **4** PEOPLE

4 artichokes
2 lemons
4 oz. (120 g) Parmigiano Reggiano cheese, shaved
1/4 cup (50 ml) extra-virgin olive oil
4-5 fresh mint leaves, minced
Salt and pepper

METHOD

ean the artichokes, removing their outer leaves and thorns. Wash the stems
soak them for 15 minutes in water mixed with the juice of one lemon.
the juice of the second lemon with the extra-virgin olive oil, a pinch of salt and
ground pepper.
rtichokes in half, removing, if necessary, any stringy fibers from the inside. Cut
nto thin slices and season with the dressing.
artichokes on the middle of a plate, garnish them with the Parmigiano Reggiano
leaves, and a drizzle of extra-virgin olive oil.

Preparation time: 20' - Difficulty: easy

CHICKEN SALAD WITH PARMIGIANO REGGIANO

INGREDIENTS FOR 4 PEOPLE

7 oz. (200 g) arugula

2 sprigs of fresh rosemary

1 bay leaf

2 sprigs of fresh sage

1 clove garlic

1 cup (200 ml) balsamic vinegar

1 1/2 cups (350 ml) water

14 oz. (400 g) chicken breast, split

1/2 cup (100 ml) extra-virgin olive oil

2 oz. (50 g) pine nuts

3 1/4 oz. (80 g) Parmigiano Reggiano cheese

Salt and pepper

METHOD

ean the arugula. Wash and mince half of the rosemary, bay leaf, sage, and garlic.
bine three-quarters of the balsamic vinegar, a pinch of salt, and the unminced
in a saucepan, and cover with the water. Bring to a boil over medium heat and
chicken breasts. Simmer for about 20 minutes. When done, let the chicken
ol in the liquid.

icken into strips and marinate them in a dash of oil and the minced herbs for
utes.

nuts in a pan over a medium flame without letting them brown too much.
the rest of the balsamic vinegar with the olive oil and a pinch of salt and pepper.
iano Reggiano cheese into thin slivers with an appropriate utensil.
rugula in the center of each plate and drizzle with the dressing. Arrange chicken
inkle with the toasted pine nuts and Parmigiano shavings.
a few drops of dressing.

Preparation time: 15' - Marinating time: 15'
Cooking time: 20' - Difficulty: easy

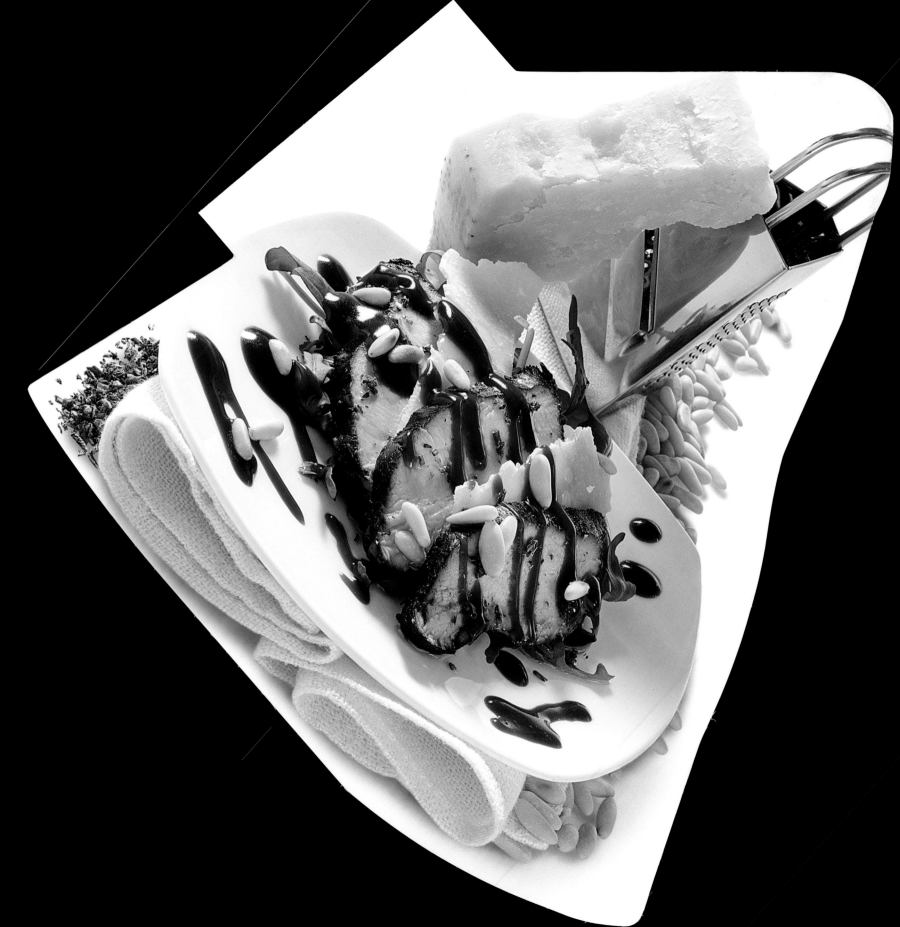

PARMIGIANO REGGIANO MOUSSE WITH BRESAOLA

INGREDIENTS FOR 4 PEOPLE

1 cup (200 ml) cream
2 gelatin leaves, softened in cold water
3 oz. (80 g) Parmigiano Reggiano cheese, grated
4 oz. (120 g) bresaola
Juice of 1 lemon
4 tbsp. (60 ml) extra-virgin olive oil
Mixed greens
1 stalk of celery, finely chopped
Traditional balsamic vinegar from Modena, as needed
Salt and pepper

METHOD

ng the cream to a boil in a saucepan. Stir in the softened gelatin until it dis-
es, then add the grated Parmigiano Reggiano. Let cool.
ge the bresaola on a plate. Drizzle with a dressing prepared by whisking the
uice and olive oil with a pinch of salt and freshly ground pepper.
vith the mixed greens, celery, and the Parmigiano Reggiano mousse, squeezed
oastry bag or shaped into *quenelles* with two spoons.
a few drops of balsamic vinegar.

Preparation time: 30' - Difficulty: easy

FRIED PUFF PASTRY POCKETS WITH PARMIGIANO REGGIANO CREAM

INGREDIENTS FOR 4 PEOPLE

2 tbsp. (25 g) butter
1 oz. (25 g) flour
1/2 cup (100 ml) milk
5 oz. (140 g) Parmigiano Reggiano cheese, grated
3 sheets of phyllo dough
2 tbsp. (30 g) butter, melted
Oil, for frying

METHOD

Melt the butter in a saucepan, add the flour and cook for a couple of minutes, making sure that the mixture does not brown.
Add the milk, bring to a boil and continue cooking for a minute or two. Let the mixture cool, and then add the grated Parmigiano Reggiano. Salt to taste, if necessary.
Brush the sheets of phyllo dough with the melted butter. Cut into squares, fill with the cooled fondue, and shape into rolls or pockets, making sure to seal the filling thoroughly.
Deep fry in oil, or bake in the oven for 15 minutes at 390 oF (200 oC).

Preparation time: 30' - Cooking time: 15'
Difficulty: medium

PARMIGIANO REGGIANO *SFORMATINO*

INGREDIENTS FOR 4 PEOPLE

1 cup (250 ml) light cream
1/3 oz. (10 g) cornmeal,
   moistened in a spoonful of cold water
2 eggs, beaten
3 1/2 oz. (100 g) Parmigiano Reggiano cheese, grated
Salt and pepper

METHOD

Scald the cream in a pot, and then add the moistened cornmeal. Mix well and let cool for several minutes.

Add the beaten eggs to the mixture, then the grated Parmigiano.

Grease individual molds and fill them with the mixture up to half an inch below the rim.

For the water bath, set the molds into a baking dish with a tall rim. Add water to baking dish, being careful not to get water into the molds. Bake at 300 ºF (150 ºC) for about 20 minutes. Allow to set for several minutes, then remove from molds and serve.

DID YOU KNOW...

You can serve this *sformatino* with a crispy Parmigiano Reggiano flower. On a sheet of parchment paper, spread and flatten a tablespoonful of grated cheese into the shape of a circle. Place in a microwave for one minute or as long as the cheese is not completely melted. Remove the sheet from the oven, taking care not to burn yourself with the melted cheese—it will be scorching hot. Wait a few seconds, and then mold the wafer, holding it firmly at the center and bending it at the edges until it assumes the appearance of a flower.

Preparation time: 20' - Cooking time: 20'
Difficulty: easy

BAKED PARMIGIANO REGGIANO WITH TRUFFLES

INGREDIENTS FOR 4 PEOPLE

5 1/4 oz. (150 g) Parmigiano Reggiano cheese
1 1/2 tbsp. (20 g) butter
1 medium truffle

METHOD

...ave the Parmigiano Reggiano into very thin slices with the appropriate tool.
...ter four individual baking dishes thoroughly. Place a slice of the Parmigiano Reg-
... in each, then a sliver of truffle, then cover these with another slice of Parmi-
...Reggiano and continue in this manner until all the ingredients have been used.
... the cheese.
... few minutes at 350ºF (180ºC) until the Parmigiano Reggiano begins to melt.
...diately.

...no cheese and truffles, two indisputable champions of Italian gastronomical culture,
...that go perfectly together. A harmonious couple, in other words, that is at best in dish-
... in terms of ingredients and preparation, but delicious in flavor and aroma, such as fried
...eggiano and truffles. After whipping two egg whites in a bowl nearly into snow, fry them
...when they are almost done cooking, add the two yolks to the middle of the frying whites,
...d out from them and remain somewhat soft. Remove the eggs from the flame, arrange a
...giano and some slivers of truffles on them, season with salt, and serve very hot.

Preparation time: 10' - Cooking time: 5'
Difficulty: easy

SPINACH AND PARMIGIANO REGGIANO SAVORY PIE

INGREDIENTS FOR **4** PEOPLE

2 tbsp. (25 ml) extra-virgin olive oil
1 clove garlic, peeled
9 oz. (250 g) spinach
7 oz. (200 g) puff pastry
1 tbsp. (15 g) cornmeal
2/3 cup (150 ml) milk
1 egg
2 1/2 oz. (70 g) Parmigiano Reggiano cheese, grated
Salt and pepper

METHOD

ur the olive oil into a frying pan set on medium heat. Add the whole garlic clove
 spinach. Keep cooking for about five minutes, then season with salt and pep-
t cool, and remove the garlic.
 the puff pastry to a thickness of 1/8 inch. Line a cake pan (or four individual
ith the dough.
 cornmeal with a drop or two of the milk. Prepare a mixture by beating the egg
h the milk, cornmeal, grated Parmigiano Reggiano, and salt and pepper to taste.
inach over the bottom of the pie, and then pour the filling over it. Bake at 350 ºF
minutes (lower temperature if making four individual pies).

Preparation time: 20' - Cooking time: 30'
Difficulty: easy

BREAD

PARMIGIANO REGGIANO SEASONED BREADSTICKS

INGREDIENTS FOR **4** PEOPLE

2 oz. (60 g) almonds
4 1/4 oz. (120 g) Italian type "00" or all-purpose flour
3 oz. (80 g) potato starch
7 oz. (200 g) butter, softened to room temperature
2 eggs
1 cup (100 g) Parmigiano Reggiano cheese, grated
Salt

40

METHOD

Grind the almonds with the flour in a food mill, and then add the potato starch and salt to taste.

Mix the softened butter with the eggs, add the grated Parmigiano Reggiano, and finally, the flour-almond mixture. Wrap the dough in plastic wrap and refrigerate for at least 1 hour.

Roll out the dough with a rolling pin to a thickness of 1/8 inch (you can press designs into the pastry dough with a mold) and cut into rectangles of the size desired.

Place the rectangles on a cookie sheet and bake at 350 ºF (180 ºC) for about 15 minutes. Cool the breadsticks before serving.

Preparation time: 20' - Resting time: 1 h
Cooking time: 15' - Difficulty: easy

PARMIGIANO REGGIANO SESAME ROLLS

INGREDIENTS FOR 6 PEOPLE

9 oz. (250 g) all-purpose flour
9 oz. (250 g) durum flour or semolina
2 tsp. (12 g) brewer's yeast
1 1/2 cups (350 ml) water, at room temperature
4 tsp. (20 ml) extra-virgin olive oil
1 3/4 oz. (50 g) Parmigiano Reggiano cheese, grated
Sesame seeds, as needed
Salt

METHOD

Combine the two flours on a pastry board and make a well. Crumble the yeast in the water until dissolved, then pour into the well and begin kneading. Mix in the olive oil and the grated Parmigiano Reggiano. End with a pinch of salt and continue kneading until the dough is soft, uniform, and elastic. Then shape it into nuggets Wrap the dough in food wrap and let rest for about 10 minutes. Then shape it into nuggets of about 1 1/3 oz. (40 g).

Lightly moisten the balls and sprinkle them with a thin layer of sesame seeds, then place them on a cookie sheet lined with parchment paper and let them rise, covered with a dishtowel, for about one hour.

Bake at 350°F (180°C) for about 20 minutes.

Preparation time: 10' - Rising time: 1 h 10'
Cooking time: 20' - Difficulty: medium

BORLENGO

INGREDIENTS FOR 4 PEOPLE

2 oz. (60 g) lard
1 sprig fresh rosemary
1 clove garlic
2 cups (250 g) all-purpose flour
4 1/4 cups (1 L) water
1 egg
3 1/2 oz. (100 g) butter, and as needed
1 cup (100 g) Parmigiano Reggiano cheese, grated
Salt

44   **METHOD**

Mince the lard with the garlic and rosemary.
Mix the flour, water, egg, and salt together until you have a smooth batter.
Allow to rest at least 1 hour.
Prepare the *borlengo* by pouring the mixture into a very hot tin-plated copper frying pan greased with butter (traditionally greased with pork rind), spreading it with the back of a spoon. After a few seconds, when it has congealed, flip it over and finish cooking.
Spread the center of each borlengo with the lard mash, which will soften it; then sprinkle the grated Parmigiano Reggiano on top.
Fold in quarters and serve immediately.

Preparation time: 10' - Resting time: 1 h
Cooking time: 5' - Difficulty: medium

PARMIGIANO REGGIANO AND PAPRIKA CRACKERS

INGREDIENTS FOR 4-6 PEOPLE

2 cups (250 g) flour
1 oz. (25 g) Parmigiano Reggiano cheese, grated
Sweet paprika, to taste
1/2 tbsp. (5 g) brewer's yeast
1/2 tsp. (2 1/2 g) malt or honey
1/2 cup (125 ml) water
1 tbsp. (13 ml) extra-virgin olive oil
Salt

METHOD

ombine the flour, grated Parmigiano Reggiano, and paprika on a pastry board
make a well in the middle. Crumble the yeast into the well and begin to knead,
g the malt, and, little by little, the water. End with the oil and salt, until you have
ugh.
dough in food wrap, and let rest for about one hour. Then roll out to a thickness
16 inch, and cut into desired shapes (diamonds, squares, etc.).
ackers on baking sheets lined with parchment paper and let rest for 10 minutes.
F (180ºC) for 15 minutes.

Preparation time: 30' - Resting time: 1 h 10'
Cooking time: 15' - Difficulty: medium

PARMIGIANO REGGIANO PINWHEELS

INGREDIENTS FOR 4 PEOPLE

For the dough
4 cups (500 g)
Italian type "00"
or all-purpose flour
3/4 oz. (20 g) sugar
1 egg
3/4 oz. (20 g) brewer's yeast,
dissolved in 1 cup (250 ml)
water

1 oz. (25 g butter), softened
to room temperature
Salt

For the garnish
2 oz. (60 g) Parmigiano
Reggiano cheese, grated
1 egg, beaten

METHOD

lake a well in the flour on a pastry board. Add the sugar, egg, and, little by little,
water in which the yeast has been dissolved. Add the butter and salt, and con-
kneading until the dough is smooth and elastic.
the bowl with plastic wrap and allow the dough to rest in a warm and humid
r around 30 minutes.
lling pin, roll out the dough on a floured pastry board to a thickness of 1/8 inch.
nish, brush the dough with part of the beaten egg and sprinkle with the grated
eggiano. Roll the dough into a long loaf and cut into slices 3/4-inch thick.
ered baking sheet and let rise until the slices double in volume (usually around one

of the pinwheels with the remaining beaten egg and bake in an oven at 390-425ºF
und 20 minutes.

Preparation time: 1 h - Rising time: 1 h 30'
Cooking time: 20' - Difficulty: difficult

BRIOCHE WITH PARMIGIANO REGGIANO

INGREDIENTS FOR 4 PEOPLE

3 eggs
6 oz. (170 g) Parmigiano Reggiano, grated
6 tbsp. (75 g) butter, melted
2 tbsp. (25 g) brewer's yeast, dissolved in 1/2 cup (100 ml) lukewarm water

3/4 lb. (325 g) flour
1/2 tbsp. (7 g) baking powder
Butter, as needed
2 oz. (50 g) breadcrumbs
1 egg, beaten
Salt and pepper

METHOD

a bowl, beat the eggs with a pinch of salt, a dash of freshly ground pepper, and 4 ounces (150 g) of the grated Parmigiano Reggiano. Stir in the melted butter he water with dissolved brewer's yeast. Add the flour and baking powder, and

and sprinkle with breadcrumbs four individual baking molds, of a size used to he caramel (or a plum-cake mold), and fill each halfway with dough.
gh rise until double in volume (it will take about an hour), then brush the surface en egg. Sprinkle with the grated Parmigiano Reggiano and some freshly ground he *pan brioche* in a preheated oven at 350ºF (180ºC) for about 40 minutes.

Preparation time: 30' - Rising time: 1 h
Cooking time: 40' - Difficulty: easy

SPINACH
AND PARMIGIANO
REGGIANO LOAF

INGREDIENTS FOR A 1 3/4- LB. LOAF

4 cups (500 g) flour
3 1/2 oz. (100 g) Parmigiano Reggiano cheese, grated
3 1/2 oz. (100 g) spinach, puréed and strained
Nutmeg, to taste
2 tsp. (12 g) brewer's yeast, crumbled
1-1/8 cups (275 ml) water
2 tbsp. (25 g) butter, softened
Salt

METHOD

On a pastry board, make a well in the flour, then add the grated Parmigiano Reggiano, the spinach purée, a pinch of nutmeg, and the crumbled yeast. Begin to knead, adding the water little by little. End by kneading in the softened butter and salt until the dough is medium-soft.

Let the dough rest in a warm place, covered with plastic wrap for about 15 minutes. Then place in a loaf pan and let rise for another 45 minutes.

Bake at 350ºF (180ºC) for about 40 minutes.

Preparation time: 30' - Rising time: 1 h
Cooking time: 40' - Difficulty: medium

PIZZA WITH ARUGULA AND PARMIGIANO REGGIANO

INGREDIENTS FOR 4 PEOPLE

For the dough
4 cups (500 g)
soft flour
1 1/2 cups (350 ml) water,
at room temperature
2 tsp. (10 g) brewer's yeast
for 2-hour rising time (1 tsp.
(4 g) for 5-6 hour rising time)
1 1/2 tbsp. (20 ml)

extra-virgin olive oil
Salt

For the topping
1 carton tomatoes, peeled
14 oz. (400 g) mozzarella, shredded
3 1/2 oz. (100 g) arugula,
finely chopped
5 1/4 oz. (150 g) Parmigiano Reggiano
cheese, shaved

METHOD

ake a well in the flour on a pastry board. Pour in the water, into which the yeast
been crumbled and dissolved, and begin kneading. Add the oil and finally the salt.
nue working the dough until it is soft, smooth, and elastic.
the dough with oil, cover it with plastic wrap, and let rest for 10 minutes. Then gen-
out on a baking sheet, greased with oil. Imagine you are playing the piano and, us-
ur fingertips, stretch the dough out to cover the entire baking sheet
h rise for 40 minutes if you have used 2 tsp. of yeast. If you have used 1 tsp., place
et, covered with plastic wrap, in the refrigerator for at least 5-6 hours. The dough
y well in the refrigerator and be light and aromatic.
d the peeled tomatoes and mozzarella (making sure they are at room temperature)

hed the pizza, let it rise for another 40 minutes or so, then bake at 425ºF (220ºC) for

oven, garnish with the arugula and shaved Parmigiano Reggiano (likewise at room tem-

Preparation time: 15' - Rising time: about 2-7 h
Cooking time: 20' - Difficulty: medium

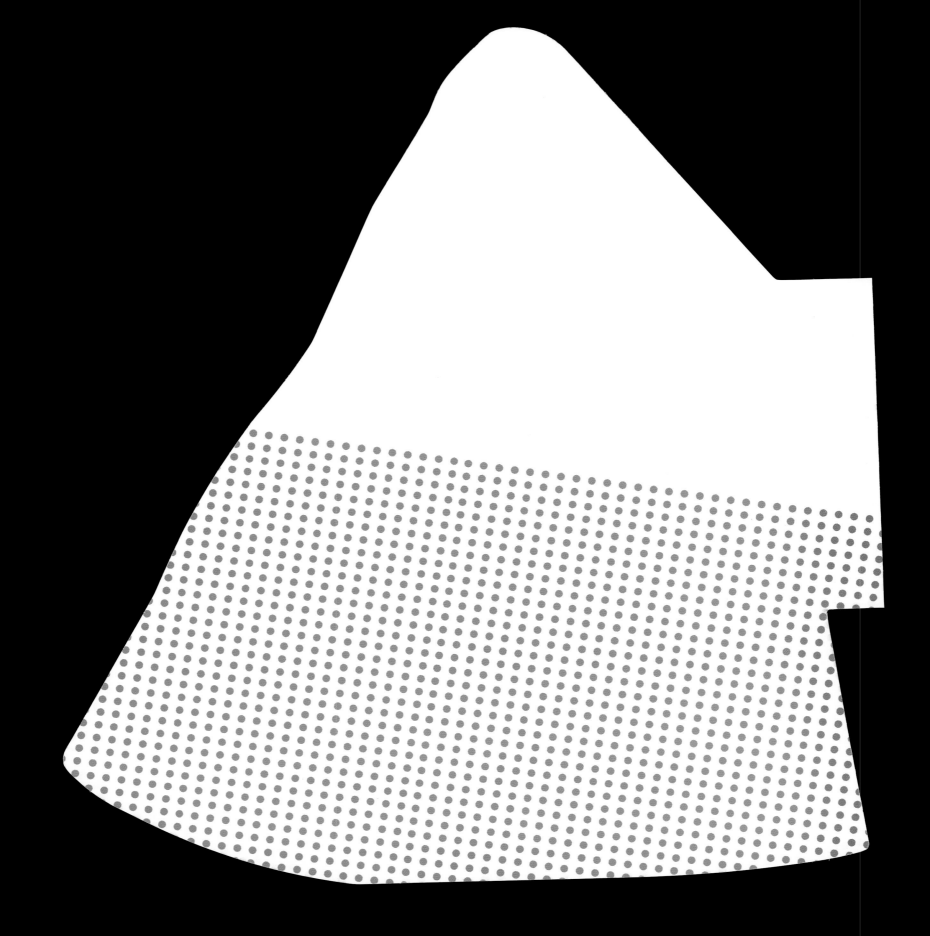

FIRST COURSES

CRÊPES WITH ASPARAGUS AND PARMIGIANO REGGIANO FONDUE

INGREDIENTS FOR 4-6 PEOPLE

For the crêpes
3 eggs
1 1/4 cups (300 ml) milk
1 cup (125 g) Italian type "00" or all-purpose flour
1 1/2 tbsp. (20 g) butter, melted
Extra-virgin olive oil
Salt

For the filling
18 oz. (500 g) asparagus
7 oz. (200 g) ricotta
1 3/4 oz. (50 g) Parmigiano Reggiano cheese, grated

Nutmeg, salt and pepper

For the Parmigiano Reggiano fondue
1/2 tsp. (3 g) butter
1 1/2 tbsp. (20 g) flour
1 1/4 cups (300 ml) milk
4 1/4 oz (120 g) Parmigiano Reggiano cheese, grated
Salt

For the gratin
1 1/2 tbsp. (20 g) butter
1 1/2 oz. (40 g) Parmigiano Reggiano cheese, grated

METHOD

Using a whisk, beat the eggs in a bowl with the milk, flour, and salt to taste. Stir in the melted butter. Cover and let rest in the refrigerator.Wash the asparagus; trim the stalks, discarding the tough ends. Cook in salted boiling water with tips facing upwards, making sure that they stay upright. Set a non-stick frying pan over a medium flame; grease it lightly and pour in a ladleful of the crêpe batter. As soon as the batter begins to set, flip it over to the other side. Repeat the operation until all the batter is gone. For the fondue, melt the butter in a saucepan. Add the flour and let it cook for a couple of minutes without letting it brown. Add the milk, bring to a boil and keep cooking for 1-2 minutes. Let cool, then add the grated Parmigiano Reggiano, and salt to taste, if necessary. Cut the asparagus into chunks and combine with the ricotta, which has been broken down with a spoon. Add the grated Parmigiano Reggiano and season with the nutmeg and pepper. If necessary, salt to taste. Stuff the crêpes with the filling and fold as you wish (into quarters or rolls). Butter a baking sheet. Pour in half the crêpes and arrange the crêpes over it. Spoon the rest of the sauce over them and top with the grated Parmigiano Reggiano and a few pats of butter. Broil in the oven at 350°F (180°C) for 15 minutes.

Preparation time: 45' - Resting time: 1 h
Cooking time: 15' - Difficulty: medium

BUTTERED FETTUCCINE WITH PARMIGIANO REGGIANO

INGREDIENTS FOR 4 PEOPLE

2/3 lb. (300 g) Italian type "00" or all-purpose flour
3 eggs
6 1/2 oz. (180 g) butter, melted
3 oz. (80 g) Parmigiano Reggiano, grated
Salt

METHOD

Knead together the flour and the eggs until they are thoroughly blended and the dough is smooth. Cover with food wrap and let rest for at least 20-30 minutes.
Once the dough has rested, put it through a pasta machine and roll out into thin sheets.
Cut these into fettuccine, 1/3 to 1/2 inch wide.
Cook the fettuccine in a large pot of boiling salted water.
Drain the pasta, reserving about 1/4 cup of the cooking water. Season the pasta with the melted butter and grated Parmigiano Reggiano, mixing in a spoonful of the cooking water.
Serve immediately.

Preparation time: 45' - Resting time: 20-30'
Cooking time: 5' - Difficulty: easy

PARMIGIANO REGGIANO GNOCCHI AU GRATIN

INGREDIENTS FOR **4** PEOPLE

For the pasta
1 cup (250 ml) water
1 cup (125 g) flour, sifted
4 tbsp. (50 g) butter, diced
2 oz. (60 g) Parmigiano Reggiano cheese, grated
3 eggs
Salt

For the béchamel
2 tbsp. (25 g) butter
1 1/2 tbsp. (20 g) flour
1 cup (250 ml) milk, warmed
Nutmeg, to taste
Salt

For the topping
3 tbsp. (40 g) butter
3 oz. (80 g) Parmigiano Reggiano cheese, grated

METHOD

For the béchamel, melt the butter in a small pot and add the flour. Whisk the mixture until the batter is smooth and well blended. Pour in the warm milk and continue whisking to prevent lumps from forming. Salt to taste, flavor with nutmeg, and let cook for several minutes over medium heat. Allow to cool.

In a pot, combine the water, diced butter and a pinch of salt. Bring to a boil, and pour in all the sifted flour at once, beating constantly with a whisk. When the mixture has thickened, exchange the whisk for a wooden spoon and continue cooking over moderate heat for 2-3 minutes, until the mixture separates from the sides of the pot. Continue cooking, and then mix in the eggs, one by one. Add the grated Parmigiano Reggiano.

Bring a pot of salted water to a boil. Using a pastry bag fit with a large plain nozzle (about 2/3 inch in diameter) force the prepared batter into the boiling water in one long coil.

Boil this coil for a few minutes. Drain with a slotted spoon and allow to cool on a kitchen towel. Cut into large chunks the size of potato gnocchi.

Butter a casserole dish or individual baking dishes; cover the bottom with a bit of béchamel and arrange the gnocchi on top, pouring more béchamel over them. Sprinkle with lots of grated Parmigiano Reggiano and dot with the remaining butter.

Bake at 350ºF (180ºC) for around 15 minutes. Serve immediately.

Preparation time: 40' - Cooking time: 15'
Difficulty: medium

RIGATONI WITH PARMIGIANO REGGIANO CREAM

INGREDIENTS FOR **4** PEOPLE

12 oz. (350 g) rigatoni
1 1/4 cup (300 ml) cream
4 1/4 oz. (120 g) Parmigiano Reggiano cheese, grated
Traditional balsamic vinegar from Modena
Salt and pepper

METHOD

Cook the rigatoni in a potful of salted boiling water.

Meanwhile, in a saucepan, bring the cream to a simmer and add the grated Parmigiano Reggiano. Mix constantly until the mixture reaches the consistency of a thick cream. Season with salt and pepper. Keep warm.

Drain the rigatoni as soon as they are cooked *al dente*, then pour them into the saucepan with the Parmigiano Reggiano cream and stir until they are well coated.

Serve with a few drops of traditional balsamic vinegar from Modena.

DID YOU KNOW...

Along with spaghetti, rigatoni is the type of pasta that best represents Italian cooking to the rest of the world. Generally produced from durum wheat flour and water, they are hollow tubes of about 2 1/2 inches in length, cut straight rather than on a diagonal at the ends, and have longitudinal grooves on their surface (if the grooves are spiral, then they are tortiglioni; if the overall shape is bowed rather than straight, then sedani or sedanini, and if the bow is particularly accentuated, lumaconi). Thanks to their particularly "ridged" texture, which is marvelous at trapping sauce, rigatoni, are perfect for those with a cream or meat base, or for making baked noodle dishes. They appear most frequently in recipes from central and southern Italy.

Preparation and cooking time: 11' - Difficulty: easy

RISOTTO WITH PARMIGIANO REGGIANO AND RED WINE REDUCTION

INGREDIENTS FOR 4 PEOPLE

2 tbsp. (25 ml) extra-virgin olive oil
2 oz. (50 g) onion
3/4 lb. (320 g) rice
1/4 cup (50 ml) white wine
6 1/3 cups (1.5 L) vegetable broth, heated
2 tbsp. (25 g) butter
3 1/2 oz. (100 g) Parmigiano Reggiano cheese, grated
Salt

For the red wine reduction
1 cup (250 ml) red wine
1 scallion
1 sprig of fresh rosemary
1 sprig of fresh thyme
1 juniper berry
2 tsp. (10 g) cornstarch, or extra-fine cornmeal, dissolved in a bit of cold water
1 1/2 tbsp. (20 g) sugar
Salt and pepper

METHOD

To make the reduction, cook the wine with the sugar, scallion, rosemary, thyme, and juniper berry until the liquid is reduced by half. Thicken with the dissolved cornstarch (or cornmeal), and pour through a sieve. Adjust the flavor with sugar, salt, and pepper, if necessary.

Meanwhile, heat the oil in a pan. Finely chop the onion and sauté it in the oil until browned, then add the rice and let it toast for about two minutes.

Pour in the white wine, and continue cooking until it absorbs.

Add the heated broth little by little, stirring frequently and letting the rice absorb it.

As soon as it is done, remove from stove, stir in the butter and grated Parmigiano Reggiano until the risotto is creamy. Season with salt, if necessary. Serve with a drizzle of the red wine reduction.

Preparation time: 10' - Cooking time: 18'
Difficulty: medium

SPAGHETTI ALLA CHITARRA WITH PARMIGIANO REGGIANO

INGREDIENTS FOR 4 PEOPLE

2/3 lb. (300 g) Italian type "00" flour
or all-purpose flour
3 eggs
7 oz. (200 g) Parmigiano Reggiano cheese, grated
1/2 cup (100 ml) extra-virgin olive oil
Black, red, and white pepper, coarsely ground
Salt

METHOD

On a pastry board, knead together the flour, eggs, and salt to taste until the ingredients are thoroughly blended and the dough is smooth.

Cover in food wrap and let rest in the refrigerator for 30 minutes.

Once rested, roll the dough through a pasta machine into sheets. Cut the sheets into spaghetti with a *chitarra* (literally: guitar), a special wooden instrument with tightly strung wires that cuts sheets of pasta into quadrangular macaroni when a rolling pin is rolled back and forth over it.

Cook the spaghetti alla chitarra in lots of boiling salted water.

When the pasta is cooked *al dente*, remove it from the heat and drain thoroughly, reserving about 1/2 cup of the cooking water. Toss the drained pasta with the grated Parmigiano Reggiano that has been mixed with the oil and two or three tablespoons of cooking water. Season with the black, red, and white pepper to taste, making sure that all three types are coarsely ground. Serve immediately.

Preparation time: 30' - Resting time: 30'
Cooking time: 5' - Difficulty: easy

ROMAN STRACCIATELLA

INGREDIENTS FOR 4 PEOPLE

4 eggs
2 oz. (50 g) Parmigiano Reggiano cheese, grated
4 1/2 cups (1 L) beef broth
Salt

METHOD

eak the eggs into a mixing bowl and stir in the grated Parmigiano Reggiano.
g the beef broth to a boil and pour in the egg mixture.
ok for 1-2 minutes, while beating with a whisk.
to taste with salt before serving.

OW...

alla romana, which as it names implies, is typical of Roman cuisine, seems to be
but is, in fact, traditionally served at birthday celebrations in the capital because
an easy but delicious thing to prepare. Historically speaking, like warm appetizers,
its delicious strips floating in broth, has always been served at the opening of im-
uch as those in honor of nuptials or baptism, and to launch Sunday afternoon din-
trattorie. Stracciatella alla romana is normally made with Christmas broth and, as a
avorful. If a handful of Parmigiano Reggiano and eggs are added as well (there is a
lia Romagna, in which chopped greens, such as spinach or Swiss chard are combined
to understand why its flavor is still a great classic to this day.

Preparation time: 10' - Cooking time: 1-2'
Difficulty: easy

TORTELLI WITH POTATO AND PARMIGIANO REGGIANO FILLING

INGREDIENTS FOR **4** PEOPLE

For the pasta
2/3 lb. (300 g) flour
3 eggs

For the filling
14 oz. (400 g) potatoes
5 1/4 oz. (150 g) Parmigiano
Reggiano cheese, grated
Nutmeg, to taste
Salt

For the sauce
3 1/2 tbsp. (50 g) butter
Thyme, to taste
2 oz. (60 g) Parmigiano
Reggiano cheese, grated
Salt

METHOD

…ead the flour with the eggs on a flat working surface. Cover the dough in food
… and let rest in the refrigerator for at least 30 minutes.

… the potatoes in their skins in boiling salted water. When they are done, peel
…e them through a potato ricer. Combine the purée with the grated Parmigiano
…, a pinch of salt, and a twist of grated nutmeg.

… chilled dough and, with a rolling pin or pasta machine, roll out a sheet around
…ck.

… bag, squeeze out the filling into little mounds the size of a hazelnut, about 3 1/4
…one sheet of dough. Once you have finished, lay another sheet of dough over the
…rrated pastry cutter cut out the tortelli into squares of about 2 1/2 inches per side.
…, pressing down with the tines of a fork, if necessary, to prevent the filling from es-

…e butter with the thyme.
…of boiling, salted water. After 3-4 minutes, scoop them out one by one with a slotted
…ctly into the pan to fry in the thyme butter. Sprinkle with the grated Parmigiano Reg-

Preparation time: 1 h - Resting time: 30'
Cooking time: 3-4' - Difficulty: medium

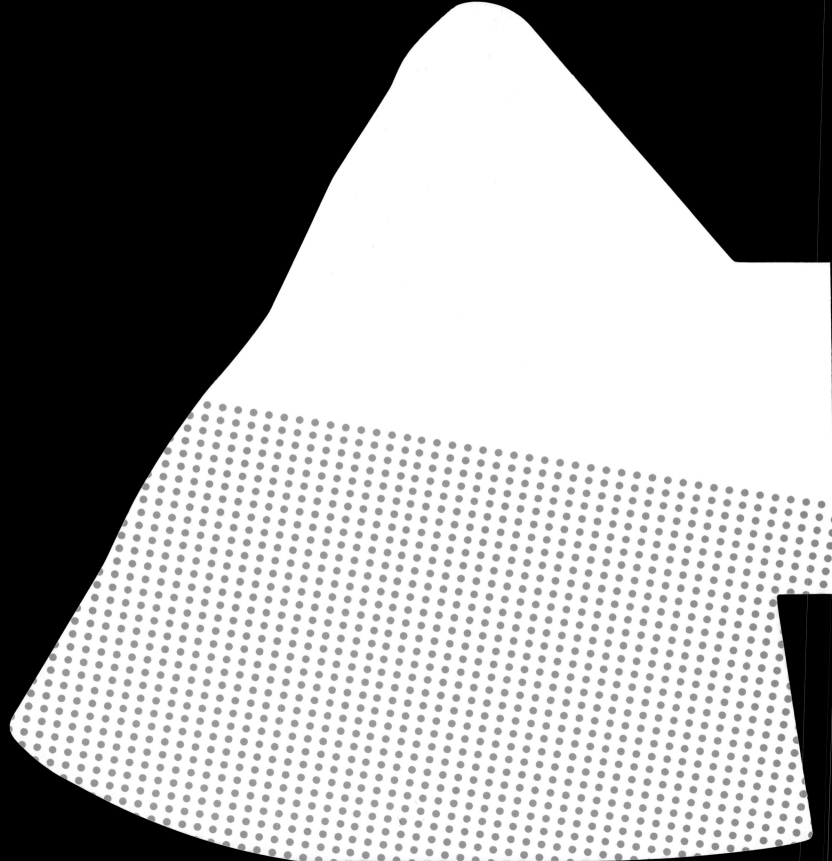

MAIN COURSES

ASPARAGUS WITH PARMIGIANO REGGIANO

INGREDIENTS FOR 4 PEOPLE

1 lbs. (800 g) asparagus
2 cups (100 g) Parmigiano Reggiano cheese, grated
4 tbsp. (60 g) butter, melted
Salt

METHOD

sh and trim the asparagus, discarding the tough ends. Stack them with their
acing upwards, and boil in salted water for about 15 minutes, making sure that
o not fall over and remain slightly firm. Drain, and then lay the stalks flat in a
dish.
he asparagus tips with the grated Parmigiano Reggiano. Meanwhile, melt the
bubbly, and pour over the asparagus.

derives its name from the Persian "asparag," or "shoot," and was later modified
oharagos," is one of the most highly prized vegetables in Italian cuisine. It is used
hes, but also for appetizers and first courses. In Italy, various types of asparagus
appearance, flavor, and manner of cultivation. They do not come only in green. The
ume this color because they sprout entirely underground, without light, which thus
ction of chlorophyll. Purple asparagus, on the other hand, are white asparagus,
o sprout from the soil, have begun the process of photosynthesis and thus acquired

Preparation time: 30' - Cooking time: 15'
Difficulty: easy

POTATO CROQUETTES WITH PARMIGIANO REGGIANO

INGREDIENTS FOR 4 PEOPLE

18 oz. (500 g) potatoes
3 1/2 tbsp. (50 g) butter
2 egg yolks
5 1/4 oz. (150 g) Parmigiano Reggiano, grated
Nutmeg, to taste

1 3/4 oz. (50 g) flour
1 egg, beaten
3 1/2 oz. (100 g) breadcrumbs
Rosemary, finely chopped
Thyme, finely chopped
Parsley, finely chopped
Oil, for frying
Salt

METHOD

Wash and cook the potatoes in lightly salted boiling water. Once they are ready, squeeze them through a potato ricer into a bowl.

Blend the potatoes with the butter, yolks, and grated Parmigiano Reggiano, and add salt and nutmeg to taste.

Spoon the mixture into balls the size of an egg, and shape into cylinders or patties. Dip first in the flour, then the beaten egg, and finally in the breadcrumbs combined with the finely chopped herbs.

Fry the croquettes in lots of boiling oil. Drain on paper towels when done. Salt to taste.

Preparation time: 30' - Cooking time: 6'
Difficulty: easy

PORK FILLET WITH PARMIGIANO REGGIANO

INGREDIENTS FOR 4 PEOPLE

For the fillet
3 1/2 oz. (100 g) caul fat
14 oz. (400 g) pork fillet
1 3/4 oz. (50 g) lard
Fresh sage, as needed
Fresh rosemary, as needed
1/2 clove garlic
2 tbsp. (30 ml) extra-virgin olive oil
1 1/2 tbsp. (20 g) butter
1/2 cup (100 ml) Marsala

Salt and pepper

For the Parmigiano Reggiano topping
3 1/2 tbsp. (50 g) butter, softened
2 tbsp. (25 g) flour
2 tbsp. (25 g) bread crumbs
1 3/4 oz. (50 g) Parmigiano Reggiano, grated
3/4 oz. (25 g) egg whites
Salt and pepper

METHOD

For the topping, mix the softened butter in a bowl with the flour, breadcrumbs, grated Parmigiano Reggiano, and egg white, and season with salt and pepper to taste. Cover the mixture in food wrap and shape into a cylindrical form thicker in diameter than the pork fillet. Refrigerate.

In the meantime, rinse the caul fat under running water and cut into four parts.

Chop the sage, rosemary, and garlic together with the lard to create a thick paste.

Cut the fillet into four medallions. Season these with salt and pepper, and rub with the paste.

Wrap each of the medallions in a piece of caul fat. Brown the medallions in oil and butter for a few minutes on each side, and then transfer to a roasting pan. Place a slice of the already prepared Parmigiano Reggiano topping on each piece.

Bake at 350-390ºF (180-200ºC) for about 10-15 minutes (increase or decrease the time based on how well done you prefer your meat).

Meanwhile, discard the excess fat from the pan and pour in the Marsala to deglaze the remaining food particles. Serve the fillet medallions with the Marsala sauce.

Preparation time: 30' - Cooking time: 10-15'
Difficulty: medium

POTATO FLAN WITH PARMIGIANO REGGIANO

INGREDIENTS FOR 4 PEOPLE

15 oz. (450 g) potatoes, boiled
1 cup (200 ml) cream
3 egg yolks
1/2 cup (50 g) Parmigiano Reggiano cheese, grated
2 1/2 tbsp. (35 g) cornstarch (or extra-fine cornmeal), dissolved in 2 tbsp. water
1 1/2 tbsp. (20 g) butter, melted
Salt and pepper

METHOD

Press the boiled potatoes through a potato ricer, and mix with the cream, yolks, grated Parmigiano Reggiano and dissolved cornstarch (or cornmeal), then season with salt and pepper to taste.

Grease suitable individual molds with the butter. Fill them 3/4 full with the potato mixture, and bake at 340oF (170C) for approximately 20 minutes.

Let cool for five minutes before removing from molds.

DID YOU KNOW...

When potatoes arrived in Europe in the mid-16th century, the belief spread—especially among the poorest ranks of society—that they were endowed with diabolical properties because they grew underground. No wonder, then, that they were held responsible for many grave diseases. However, from the late 17th century on, rulers of various European countries waged campaigns to enhance the reputation of the poor potato in order to combat frequent famines. The most astute of these was Frederick II of Prussia, who, in order to encourage people to befriend the despised tubers, came up with the idea of mounting guards in fields where they were cultivated, and thus to rouse the curiosity of the region's farmers, who began regarding them as "precious" and started stealing them both to eat and plant.

Preparation time: 40' - Cooking time: 20'
Resting time: 5' - Difficulty: easy

BOLOGNESE-STYLE ROULADES

INGREDIENTS FOR 4 PEOPLE

3/4 lb. (350 g)
veal shank
8 slices prosciutto
di Parma
3 1/2 oz. (100 g)
Parmigiano Reggiano
cheese, grated
2 tbsp. (30 ml) extra-virgin
olive oil

1 whole clove garlic,
peeled
2 sprigs fresh sage
2 sprigs fresh rosemary
1 bay leaf
1/4 cup (50 ml) white wine
1/2 cup (100 ml) beef broth
1 3/4 oz. (50 g) crushed tomatoes
Salt and pepper

METHOD

Cut the meat into eight slices, and flatten out with a meat pounder. Place a slice of prosciutto and some finely shaved Parmigiano Reggiano on each one. Roll them up and secure with toothpicks.

Heat the oil in a pan and brown the roulades. Season with salt and pepper, and then add the peeled garlic clove and the herbs. Pour the white wine over the meat and let evaporate before adding the crushed tomatoes and broth.

Cover the pan with a lid and continue cooking on medium heat for about 15 minutes.

When the meat is done, discard the garlic clove and herbs, reduce the sauce if it is too thin (or add a little hot water or broth if too thick), and serve.

Preparation time: 20' - Cooking time: 20'
Difficulty: easy

PARMIGIANO REGGIANO OMELET

INGREDIENTS FOR 1 MEDIUM OMELET

3 eggs
3 1/2 oz. (100 g) Parmigiano Reggiano cheese, grated
1 1/2 tbsp. (20 g) butter
Salt and pepper

METHOD

In a bowl, beat the eggs with some salt, pepper, and the grated Parmigiano Reggiano.
Melt butter in a warm frying pan, and then pour in the eggs.
Stir the eggs thoroughly with a fork. As soon as the eggs begin to set, flip the omelet over onto itself by lightly shaking the pan's handle up and down.
The omelet is done when it is still soft inside.

DID YOU KNOW...

To prepare an omelet—which is made like a frittata except that it is cooked on only one side, then folded over onto itself to form a half moon seems like child play. All the same, certain rules need to be followed to make it perfect. First, the eggs must be beaten carefully, until the yolks and whites are mixed but not completely merged. Next, a correct, or rather suitable pan must be used: shallow with narrow, inclined edges (which make it easier to flip the omelet over on itself). The pan needs to be clean and dry at the beginning, and very hot at the moment the eggs are poured in. Not more than a pat of butter should be used for frying. And make sure that an active flame is burning beneath the pan the whole time that the omelet is cooking.

Preparation time: 5' - Cooking time: 10'
Difficulty: medium

PARMIGIANO REGGIANO IN CARROZZA

INGREDIENTS FOR **4** PEOPLE

For the filling
1 tbsp. (15 g) butter
1 1/3 tbsp. (20 g) flour
1/2 cup (125 ml) milk
7 oz. (200 g) Parmigiano
Reggiano cheese, grated
8 slices toasting bread
Salt

For the breading
1/2 cup (100 ml) milk
1/2 cup (100 g) flour
2 eggs
3/4 cup (150 g) breadcrumbs
Oil, for frying

METHOD

elt the butter in a saucepan, add the flour and cook for a couple of minutes
out letting it brown. Add the milk, bring to a boil and cook for another couple
utes. Continue cooking adding the grated Parmigiano Reggiano, and, if neces-
t.

crusts off the slices of bread. Using a pastry bag, squeeze a layer of the Parmi-
iano filling between two slices of bread. Press together so that the slices really
e another.

s of the sandwiches in the milk, then dip them first in the flour, then in the beat-
ally in the bread crumbs. Repeat the process a second time to ensure that the
s evenly spread.

in the oil, turning them over so that they are well browned on both sides.
s and serve hot.

Preparation time: 20' - Cooking time: 5'
Difficulty: medium

CHICKEN BREASTS WITH PARMIGIANO REGGIANO CRUST

INGREDIENTS FOR 4 PEOPLE

14 oz. (400 g) chicken breasts
Fresh parsley, as needed
Fresh thyme, as needed
2 3/4 oz. (75 g) breadcrumbs
4 1/4 oz. (120 g) Parmigiano Reggiano cheese, grated
2 tbsp. (25 g) flour
3 egg whites
Salt and pepper
Oil, for frying

METHOD

Cut the chicken breasts into four fillets (or chunks, if you prefer).
Wash, dry, and place the herbs in a food processor with the breadcrumbs and the grated Parmigiano Reggiano, and process them all together.
In a mixing bowl, beat the egg whites with salt and pepper.
Dip the chicken pieces in the flour, then the egg whites, and finally in the herbed breadcrumbs. Repeat the operation a second time to ensure an even coating.
Fry the chicken breasts in very hot oil, drain on paper towels, and serve.

DID YOU KNOW...

Thyme (thymus) has been considered an aromatic herb with unusual properties since ancient times. Its name derives from the Greek word "thymos," which signifies "power, boldness, and energy." It was christened thus because it was known to bring out this quality in those who inhaled its pleasing fragrance. In the Middle Ages, noblewomen embroidered sprigs of thyme on the insignia of knights in order to infuse their hearts with courage. This herb, used in cooking for its fragrance, is not only capable of exerting a beneficial psychological influence but also possesses antiseptic properties. No wonder that since the time of World War I it has been one of the principal ingredients of disinfectants.

Preparation time: 30' - Cooking time: 5'
Difficulty: easy

PARMIGIANO REGGIANO POTATO PIE

INGREDIENTS FOR 4 PEOPLE

14 oz. (400 g) potatoes, peeled and washed
1 cup (200 ml) whipping cream
2/3 cup (150 ml) milk
1 clove garlic
Butter, as needed
3 1/2 oz. (100 g) of Parmigiano Reggiano cheese, grated
Salt and white pepper

METHOD

Slice the peeled potatoes into very thin pieces using a mandoline or a slicing machine.

Pour the cream in a saucepan and add the milk, sliced potatoes, salt, pepper, and garlic clove. Set the saucepan on medium heat, cover with lid, and cook until the potatoes are soft. Discard the garlic clove.

Butter a baking pan or individual baking molds, and fill with the potato mixture, adding the grated Parmigiano Reggiano.

Bake at 350ºF (180ºC) for about 20 minutes until the surface is browned.

Cool (in order to cut neatly), and cut into desired shapes.

Before serving, heat in oven at 350ºF (180ºC) for a few minutes.

Preparation time: 20' - Cooking time: 20'
Difficulty: easy

SNACKS

PARMIGIANO REGGIANO BAVARIAN CREAM WITH PEARS AND WINE

INGREDIENTS FOR 4-6 PEOPLE

For the Bavarian cream

5 egg yolks
1 oz. (30 g) sugar
1 tsp. (5 g) flour
1/2 cup (125 ml) milk, scalded
1 oz. (30 g) Parmigiano Reggiano cheese, grated
1 1/2 gelatin leaves, soaked in cold water and wrung out
1/2 cup (130 g) whipped heavy cream

Butter, as needed
Salt

For the pear gelatin

14 oz. (400 g) pears
1 cup (200 ml) red wine
2 1/4 oz. (65 g) sugar
1-2 whole cloves
Cinnamon stick
1 1/2 gelatin leaves, soaked in cold water and wrung out

METHOD

For the gelatin, peel the pears, cut into chunks, and cook in a saucepan on medium heat with the wine, sugar, cloves, and a cinnamon stick. When the pears are soft, put them in a blender, adding the gelatin leaf. Blend thoroughly and pour the mixture into molds smaller than those that will be used for the Bavarian cream. Refrigerate.

For the Bavarian cream, whisk together the yolks and the sugar in a bowl; add the flour, a pinch of salt, and the scalded milk. Pour into a saucepan and bring to a boil, and continue cooking for 2-3 minutes.

Meanwhile, combine the grated Parmigiano Reggiano, the gelatin leaf soaked in cold water, and the butter. Mix well and chill. When the cream begins to congeal, delicately fold in the whipped cream, and pour into the buttered molds.

Place a set pear gelatin in each of the molds and place in the freezer for a couple of hours. Unmold the Bavarian creams and let them thaw before serving (about one hour in the refrigerator or 20 minutes at room temperature). Decorate as desired.

Preparation time: 1 h - Freezing time: 2 h
Resting time: 20'-1 h - Difficulty: difficult

PARMIGIANO REGGIANO BASKETS

INGREDIENTS FOR 4 PEOPLE

4 1/4 oz. (120 g) Parmigiano Reggiano, grated

METHOD

Create disks, 4 inches in diameter, from the grated Parmigiano by sprinkling the cheese in an even layer on a sheet of parchment paper or a silicone baking sheet.

Cook in the microwave for a minute or more, depending on the power of the oven used.

Remove the disks from the oven when the cheese is thoroughly melted. Let them cool a bit, and then invert them onto a cup or small bowl so that they assume the form of baskets.

Let chill completely, and keep in a dry place for several days.

Serve the baskets filled with mousse, salad, or some other delicacy.

DID YOU KNOW...

In October 2008, the first monument in the world dedicated to Parmigiano Reggiano, the work of the sculptor Michelangelo Galliani, was unveiled in Bibbiano (Reggio Emilia). There, in a green meadow recalling the pastures that serve as the principal source of nourishment for the cows that produce the milk for Parmigiano Reggiano, stands an enormous piece of cheese created out of marble, which, when broken open has a granular texture similar to that of Parmigiano Reggiano. Next to it, stands a wall made of terracotta with shutters arranged in staggered rows, typical of the old neo-Gothic polygonal dairies. As well as a classic short, almond-shaped knife, of the sort used for cutting the cheese.

Preparation time: 5' · Cooking time: 1'
Difficulty: easy

PARMIGIANO REGGIANO CHOCOLATES

INGREDIENTS FOR APPROXIMATELY **25** CHOCOLATES

For the chocolates
1/2 cup (100 ml) cream
3/4 oz. (20 g) glucose syrup
1 1/2 oz. (40 g) Parmigiano Reggiano cheese, grated

3 1/2 oz. (100 g) chocolate fondant, ground
25 hollow chocolate balls

For the decoration
5 1/4 oz. (150 g) chocolate fondant

METHOD

Boil the cream with the glucose syrup in a saucepan. Remove from flame and add the grated Parmigiano Reggiano. Emulsify the ingredients with a hand-held immersion blender and add most of the ground chocolate fondant. Blend carefully to obtain a velvety, smooth cream.

Let the cream cool, and then use a pastry bag to fill the hollow chocolate balls.

Let the chocolates solidify in a cool place but not a refrigerator, for approximately 12 hours. When the filling has solidified, seal the openings of the balls with the remaining melted chocolate, and let them harden.

In order to soften the chocolate fondant for the finish, melt it to a temperature of 113-120°F (45-49 °C) (use a kitchen thermometer) in a double boiler or a microwave. Then pour 1/3 to 1/2 of it on a marble surface. Let cool to a temperature of 78-80°F (25-27°C), scraping the chocolate the whole time with a spatula. Then combine it with the remaining hot topping. When it has reached a temperature of 87-89°F (30-32°C), it is ready to be used.

Re-coat the chocolates with the warm chocolate and let harden. Decorate as desired.

Preparation time: 45' - Resting time: 12 h
Difficulty: difficult

PARMIGIANO REGGIANO BUTTERFLY PUFFS

INGREDIENTS FOR 4-6 PEOPLE

7 oz. (200 g) puff pastry
2 eggs
3 oz. (80 g) Parmigiano Reggiano cheese, grated
Pepper

METHOD

Pull the puff pastry to a thickness of around 1/10 inch.
Beat the eggs in a mixing bowl with a few drops of water and a twist of freshly ground pepper. Brush the mixture thickly on the surface of the puff pastry. Top with the grated Parmigiano Reggiano, and cut into rectangles.
Twist the rectangles into the shapes of butterflies, then place on a baking sheet lined with parchment paper. Bake at 390°F (200°C) for 10-12 minutes.
Remove from oven when the Parmigiano Reggiano butterflies are perfectly golden. Serve on a platter while still hot.

Preparation time: 20' - Cooking time: 10-12'
Difficulty: easy

PARMIGIANO REGGIANO ICE CREAM

INGREDIENTS FOR APPROXIMATELY 2 LBS ICE CREAM

2 1/4 cups (500 ml) milk
6 1/2 oz. (180 g) cane sugar
3/4 oz. (20 g) powdered skim milk
1/2 oz. (15 g) dextrose
1 tsp. (5 g) ice cream stabilizer
1/2 cup (100 ml) cream
4 1/4 oz. (120 g) Parmigiano Reggiano cheese, grated

METHOD

In a saucepan, heat the milk to 115ºF (45ºC).

Mix the sugar, powdered milk, dextrose, and stabilizer, and pour the mixture all at once into milk.

Add the cream and pasteurize at 185ºF (85ºC). Add the grated Parmigiano Reggiano and cool quickly to 40ºF (4ºC) by pouring the mixture into a vessel immersed in a bucket full of water and ice.

Let the mixture rest at 40ºF (4ºC) for 6 hours, then freeze, churning it in an ice-cream maker until the mixture is foamy and dry-looking, that is, not shiny (the time will depend on the type of ice-cream-maker used).

Preparation time: 20' - Resting time: 6 h
Difficulty: easy

BATTER-FRIED PARMIGIANO REGGIANO

INGREDIENTS FOR **4-6** PEOPLE

2 eggs
1/3 lb. (160 g) flour
2/3 cup (150 ml) milk
3 cups (300 g) Parmigiano Reggiano cheese
Salt
Oil for frying

METHOD

Beat the eggs with the flour in a bowl. Add the milk to obtain a smooth batter with no lumps. Salt to taste and let rest in a cool place for an hour.
Cut the Parmigiano Reggiano into chunks, and heat up the oil in a suitable pot.
Test the density of the batter by immersing a piece of cheese into it. If necessary, dilute it with a few drops of milk.
When the oil is hot, dip the chunks of Parmigiano Reggiano in the batter, let the excess drip off and fry them until they are golden.
Drain them on paper towels and serve immediately.

Preparation time: 10' - Resting time: 1 h
Cooking time: 3-5' - Difficulty: easy

GRILLED PARMIGIANO REGGIANO

INGREDIENTS FOR 4-6 PEOPLE

14 oz. (400 g) Parmigiano Reggiano cheese rinds
Extra-virgin olive oil, for brushing

METHOD

Scrape the Parmigiano Reggiano rinds with the blade of a knife.
Cut into rectangles, brush with the extra-virgin olive oil and place on a very hot grill (or under a broiler) for a few minutes, until they begin to melt lightly and get grill marks.

DID YOU KNOW...

You can discover the identity, history, and miracles of Parmigiano Reggiano by visiting the Museo del Parmigiano Reggiano, established in 2003. Founded in Sorge a Soragna, in the province of Parma, it is housed in the historic circular 19th-century tollhouse next to the fortress of the Meli-Lupi princes, in an area full of citadels and memories bound to the figure of the Maestro, Giuseppe Verdi. A highly interesting exhibition space that offers visitors tastings, it plays the role of cultural custodian of the characteristics belonging to and traditions associated with this unique product. It retraces not only the production of the celebrated cheese with instruments used between the second half of the 19th century and the first half of the 20th century, when the tollhouse was still in use, but also its aging process, commerce, gastronomic usage, and history.

Preparation time: 10' - Cooking time: 3-5'
Difficulty: easy

PARMIGIANO REGGIANO PRESERVED IN OIL

INGREDIENTS FOR APPROXIMATELY 1 1/2-CUP

4 1/2 oz. (130 g) Parmigiano Reggiano cheese, broken into chunks
1-2 bay leaves
Hot peppers, to taste
Several juniper berries
1/2 cup (120 ml) extra-virgin olive oil

METHOD

Put the Parmigiano Reggiano chunks in a jar and add the bay leaves, hot peppers to taste, and several juniper berries.
Pour in the olive oil to cover completely, and seal the jar.
Refrigerate for a couple of days before consuming.
The cheese will keep for several weeks in the refrigerator so long as it remains covered in oil.

DID YOU KNOW...

Although Parmigiano Reggiano is a cheese, it is suitable even for people who are lactose intolerant. This is a widespread intolerance, which occurs when a person is incapable of digesting lactose, the principal sugar contained in milk, due to an insufficient amount or total lack of lactase, the enzyme that reduces lactose to simple sugars that can be absorbed by the gastro-intestinal tract. Parmigiano Reggiano contains neither lactose nor galactose (formed from lactose) because both are metabolized by lactic bacteria that grow in the hours immediately after the milk coagulates into cheese. Good news, therefore; even the lactose-intolerant can enjoy a nice flake of Parmigiano Reggiano, sprinkle a generous handful on their pasta, or use it to prepare tarts and vegetable pies, thus benefitting from its nutritional qualities, above all its high quantity of calcium, without running any risk.

Preparation time: 10' - Resting time: 48 h
Difficulty: easy

PARMIGIANO REGGIANO MINI PIZZAS

INGREDIENTS FOR **4-6 PEOPLE**

For the dough
1/3 lb. (150 g) butter
2 tsp. (12 g) superfine (caster) sugar
2 tsp. (10 g) dextrose
1 1/3 oz. (38 g) almond meal

1 egg
3 1/4 oz. (90 g) Italian type "OO" or all-purpose flour
3 oz. (80 g) potato starch

2 1/4 oz. (64 g) Parmigiano Reggiano, grated
Nutmeg, to taste

Salt

For the topping
4 oz. (120 g) crushed tomatoes
Oregano, to taste
2 oz. (60 g) Scamorza cheese, diced

Salt

METHOD

Whip the butter with the sugar, dextrose, and almond meal.
Add the egg and stir in the remaining ingredients.
Using a pastry bag, form the mini pizzas on a baking sheet lined with parchment paper.
Garnish with the crushed tomatoes seasoned with salt and oregano, and the diced Scamorza.
Bake at 410ºF (210ºC) for about 13 minutes.

DID YOU KNOW...

Age determines flavor. Parmigiano Reggiano cheese ages for 15-18 months, and ripens in the same manner as fresh seasonal fruit, such as pears, apples, grapes or strawberries. At 18 months, it is perfect cubed or shaved in a nice and nutritious salad of fresh greens. At 24 months, it is amazing grated, or shaved in thin flakes, on a first course, in soups and cream sauces, as well as in savory pies, oven-roasted vegetables, hot cheese tarts, and greens. At 24-28 months, it is best with dried fruit, such as walnuts and hazel-nuts, dried prunes or figs. At 22-30 months, it is exquisite with light entrées, such as thinly sliced raw meat or fish. And at 30-36 months? At that point Parmigiano Reggiano cheese is best wed to itself. Preferably with a few drops of traditional balsamic vinegar from Modena, which heightens its intense aroma and unmistakable flavor.

Preparation time: 30' - Cooking time: 13'
Difficulty: easy

PARMIGIANO REGGIANO POPCORN

INGREDIENTS FOR *4-6* PEOPLE

10 1/2 oz. (300 g) Parmigiano Reggiano cheese rinds

METHOD

Scrape the Parmigiano Reggiano rinds thoroughly with the blade of a knife.
Cut into little cubes of around 2/3 inch in breadth.
Place in a microwave on a sheet of parchment paper and heat on the highest setting until the pieces pop. The amount of time will vary according to the power of the microwave and the ripeness of the cheese.

DID YOU KNOW...

For the ultimate enjoyment of Parmigiano Reggiano flakes, all five senses need to be brought into play: sight, hearing, smell, taste, and touch. First of all, one must observe the structure of the flake, assessing its form, dimensions, color, and appearance. Then one must touch it in order to understand its structure and consistency, and its granularity and elasticity. To capture the aromas, from the strongest to the least perceptible ones, allowing one to be completely enveloped by them. When one finally bites into a little piece of the cheese and prepares to chew it, one must pay attention to the intensity of the basic flavors (that range in succession from sweet to salty and from sour to bitter), and after swallowing, to the emergence of aftertastes. Finally, when tasting slivers of Parmigiano Reggiano, one must also listen to the sonorous sounds that allow one to assess the friability of the cheese. In sum, this should be a multisensory experience rather than a simple tasting.

Preparation time: 10' - Cooking time: 1-3'
Difficulty: easy

SAVORY SBRISOLONA WITH PARMIGIANO REGGIANO

INGREDIENTS FOR 4-6 PEOPLE

1/2 cup (100 g) flour
2 tbsp. (25 g) extra-fine cornmeal
2 3/4 oz. (75 g) Parmigiano Reggiano, grated
6 tbsp. (75 g) butter
2 3/4 oz. (75 g) almonds (or peanuts)
1 egg yolk
Dash (0.5 g) of baking powder
Salt

METHOD

ind the almonds (or peanuts) in a food processor, saving a few whole ones to use
arnish. As when preparing the classic "crumbly" sbrisolona, that is, "roughened
e fingertip," place all the ingredients except the egg yolk in a bowl.
 as the mixture becomes sandy, add the yolk and stop kneading while the dough
ins large particles.
s dough into an 8-inch tart pan.
 the remaining almonds or peanuts and bake in an oven at 350ºF (180ºC) until the
owned. Remove from oven and serve.

Preparation time: 20' - Cooking time: 35'
Difficulty: easy

PARMIGIANO REGGIANO CARBONATED SHAKE

INGREDIENTS FOR 4-6 PEOPLE

4 1/4 oz. (120 g) Parmigiano Reggiano, grated
1 1/4 cups (300 ml) cream
1 gelatin leaf, soaked in cold water and wrung out
Salt and pepper (optional)

METHOD

Melt the grated Parmigiano Reggiano in a saucepan until it turns into a cream. Season the cream with salt and pepper, if desired, and then add the gelatin leaf. Mix well and pass through a fine sieve, then empty the contents of the bowl into a 1-pint soda siphon. Screw on the cap and load with a gas cartridge. Chill in the refrigerator for at least a couple of hours before serving.

DID YOU KNOW...

The siphon, used in the kitchen to prepare soft drinks, is one of the benchmarks of so-called "molecular" cuisine. Historically speaking, "siphon cream" (not to be confused with "siphon soda," which has been used for a long time to produce seltzer water), was used solely for whipping cream in ice cream parlors and pastry shops. It was in the early 1980s that the team at El Bulli, Ferran Adriá's legendary restaurant, thought of using the siphon for liquids other than cream, in order to see if a compound similar to whipped cream could be obtained. Thus were born various foams, delicate and impalpable as clouds, and able to offer new sensory experiences. These are not fried air, but genuine cooking: another way of tasting a dish. And they have not been demonized. Who would demonize whipped cream?

Preparation time: 10' - Resting time: 2 h
Difficulty: easy

PARMIGIANO REGGIANO AND ALMOND CHIPS

INGREDIENTS FOR 4 PEOPLE

3 1/4 oz. (90 g) Parmigiano Reggiano, grated
2 oz. (60 g) almonds
4 tbsp. (60 g) butter, softened at room temperature
1 1/2 tbsp. (20 g) potato starch
2 tsp. (10 g) super-fine sugar
1 oz. (25 g) almonds, slivered
1 teaspoon egg white
Salt and pepper

METHOD

ind the almonds with the potato starch in a food-processor.
bowl, mix the ground almonds with the softened butter, the sugar, grated
giano Reggiano, and egg white. Season with salt and pepper and work well with
en spoon.
mixture through a sieve and spread into disks, between 2 and 2 1/4 inches in di-
parchment paper or a silicone sheet, or better, flatten them out with a rolling pin.
chips with the slivered almonds and bake at 350ºF (180ºC) for about five minutes.
u remove the disks from the oven, detach them with a spatula and lay them on a
at when they cool they assume the typical form of chips.

Preparation time: 10' - Cooking time: 5'
Difficulty: easy

ALPHABETICAL
INDEX OF RECIPES

ALPHABETICAL INDEX OF INGREDIENTS

126

All the photographs are by Academia Barilla except:

©123RF: timer image, 123
©iStockphoto: pages 2, 5, 7, 125, 128